Raffi Songs to Read™

# TINGALAYO

## Illustrated by Kate Duke

Crown Publishers, Inc., New York

Published by Crown Publishers, Inc., 225 Park Avenue South, New York,
New York 10003 and represented in Canada by the Canadian MANDA Group
CROWN is a trademark of Crown Publishers, Inc.
RAFFI SONGS TO READ and SONGS TO READ are trademarks of Troubadour
Learning, a division of Troubadour Records Ltd.
Manufactured in Italy
Library of Congress Cataloging-in-Publication Data
Raffi. Tingalayo/Raffi; illustrated by Kate Duke.
Summary: While his master is not looking, Tingalayo the donkey
sneaks off to dance and sing at the fair.
1. Children's songs—West Indies. 2. Calypso (Songs, etc.)
[1. Donkeys—Fiction. 2. West Indies—Fiction. 3. Calypso (Songs, etc.)
4. Songs.] I. Duke, Kate, ill. II. Title.
PZ8.3.R124Ti 1988      88-3562
ISBN 0-517-56926-4

10 9 8 7 6 5 4 3 2 1

First Edition

Tingalayo, come, little donkey, come.

Tingalayo, come, little donkey, come.

Me donkey fast,

Me donkey slow,

Me donkey come

and me donkey go.

Me donkey fast,

Me donkey slow,

Me donkey come

and me donkey go.

Tingalayo, come, little donkey, come.

Tingalayo, come, little donkey, come.

Me donkey hee, me donkey haw,
Me donkey sleep in a bed of straw.

Me donkey hee, me donkey haw,
Me donkey sleep in a bed of straw.

Tingalayo, come, little donkey, come.

Tingalayo, come, little donkey, come.

Me donkey dance, me donkey sing,
Me donkey wearin' a diamond ring.

Me donkey dance, me donkey sing,
Me donkey wearin' a diamond ring.

Tingalayo, come, little donkey, come.

Tingalayo, come, little donkey, come.

Me donkey swim,

Me donkey ski,

Me donkey dress elegantly.
Me donkey swim,
Me donkey ski,
Me donkey dress elegantly.

Tingalayo, come, little donkey, come.

Tingalayo, come, little donkey, come.

# TINGALAYO

fast, me don- key slow, Me don- key come and me don- key go. Me don- key

fast, me don- key slow, Me don- key come and me don- key go.

2. Me donkey hee,
   Me donkey haw,
   Me donkey sleep in a bed of straw.

3. Me donkey dance,
   Me donkey sing,
   Me donkey wearin' a diamond ring.

4. Me donkey swim,
   Me donkey ski,
   Me donkey dress elegantly.